1·2·3®

THE POCKET REFERENCE

Mary Campbell

Osborne **McGraw-Hill**
Berkeley, California

Osborne **McGraw-Hill**
2600 Tenth Street
Berkeley, California 94710
U.S.A.

For information on translations and book distributors outside of
the U.S.A., please write to Osborne **McGraw-Hill** at the above
address.

1-2-3® is a trademark of Lotus Development Corporation.

1-2-3®: The Pocket Reference

567890 SPSO 898

ISBN 0-07-881304-2

CONTENTS

INTRODUCTION

This pocket guide is designed to serve as a reference for both novice and experienced 1-2-3 users. It is organized in a fashion that makes it possible to find a description of any 1-2-3 command quickly. Experienced users can use it to read about 1-2-3 commands they have not used or as a quick refresher for the more advanced 1-2-3 commands. New 1-2-3 users will want to keep it available at all times as a guide for the use of all 1-2-3 commands.

In addition to providing a quick reference for all the 1-2-3 commands, this reference includes a listing of the built-in functions and the arguments they require. A similar list is provided for all of the instructions in 1-2-3's command language. A list of the function keys and the ways to move the cursor in 1-2-3's different environments are included especially for the benefit of the new 1-2-3 user.

1-2-3 COMMANDS

► /Copy

Description: The /Copy command is the most powerful command that 1-2-3 has to offer. It copies numbers, labels, and formulas to new locations on the worksheet. It can copy one cell or many cells in a range to either a cell or a range.

Copying is a simple process. You need to tell 1-2-3 only two things: where to copy from, and where to copy to.

The From range can be one cell or many. Multiple cells to be copied can be arranged in a row, column, or rectangle. The From range can be typed, referenced with a range name, or highlighted with the cursor.

The To range defines whether you are making one or several copies and specifies the exact location where you would like these copies placed. Each duplication of the From information requires only that you include the top left cell in the To range. For example, if you were copying A1..A15 to B1..E15, then you would specify the To range as B1..E1, since only the top cell in each copy is included.

Options: The /Copy command supports four copying procedures: (1) one cell to one cell; (2) one cell to many cells; (3) a range of cells to a range that's the same size as the original range; and (4) a range of cells to a range whose size is a multiple of the original range — for example, a column of five cells can be duplicated in several additional columns of five cells. Specifying the From and To range determines what type of copying will take place.

Note: The /Copy command provides a quick solution for recalculating a range of cells. When you have recalculation set at Manual, or when your worksheet is so large that it takes a minute or two for the entire worksheet to be recalculated, you may want to recalculate just a few formulas. If you copy the cells containing the formula to be recalculated to themselves — that is, make the From and To ranges the same — these cells will be recalculated.

▶ /Data Distribution

Description: The /Data Distribution command permits you to create a frequency distribution table from the values in a range on your worksheet. This table will tell you how many values in the range fall within each of the intervals you establish. An area of the worksheet must be set aside to record the frequency intervals (bins) against which your data will be analyzed. The frequency for each bin will be placed in an adjacent column.

Using the /Data Distribution command requires some preliminary work. First, you must select a location on your worksheet for the bins. 1-2-3 will use the column to the right of the bins for the frequency numbers for each interval and the row immediately below the last bin for a count of all the values that exceed the last bin value. Second, the values you place in the bins must be in descending sequence from the top to the bottom of the column you are using.

An example will clarify how 1-2-3 assigns values to the bins. If you were to create bin values of 5, 10, and 20, the first bin would contain a count of the values in your list that are less than or equal to 5, the second bin would contain a count of values greater than 5 and less than or equal to 10, and the third bin would contain a count of values greater than 10 and less than or equal to 20. 1-2-3 would create a fourth bin for a count of all values greater than 20.

Cells containing labels or blanks will be categorized as cells that have a value of zero. Both ERR and NA are regarded as numeric values. ERR will be counted in the highest interval, since it is considered greater than all numeric values, and NA will be categorized in the first (lowest) interval, since it is considered to be lower than any other numeric value.

Once /Data Distribution has classified the values in the specified range, changing one of the values will not cause a reclassification. To reclassify data after a change, you must enter /Data Distribution again. This time, however, all you have to do is press ENTER in response to 1-2-3's prompts, since 1-2-3 will suggest the same ranges that were used last time.

Options: This command gives you only two options: the size of the intervals you enter in the bin range, and the number of values in the values range.

▶ /Data Fill

Description: The /Data Fill command allows you to produce an ascending or descending list of numbers. The numbers in the list must be separated by the same interval. The numbers in the following series can all be generated with /Data Fill:

    1 2 3 4 5 6 7 8 9 10 11 12 13 14 15 16
    5001 5006 5011 5016 5021 5026 5031 5036
    90 88 86 84 82 80 78 76 74 72 70 68 66

When you use the /Data Fill command, first you need to tell 1-2-3 the range of cells that you wish to have filled with a numeric series. Then 1-2-3 will prompt you for the three variables that provide flexibility in series generation.

Options: When you use /Data Fill, 1-2-3 will ask
you to supply a start value, a stop value, and an
increment or step value. The start value is the
beginning number in your sequence and has a
default of 0. The stop value is the last value in
your sequence. The default is 8191 or the last
number that will fit within the range selected. The
increment (step) is the distance between each pair
of numbers in the series. It has a default value of
1 and can be either positive or negative.

▶ /Data Matrix

Description: The /Data Matrix command is new in
Release 2. It allows you to perform multiplication and inversion on large matrices up to 90
rows by 90 columns.

Matrices are tabular arrangements of data
with a number in each cell. They are specified by
their size. The number of rows is specified before
the number of columns. Thus, a matrix with 5
rows and 6 columns is a 5 by 6 matrix. A square
matrix has the same number of rows as columns.

1-2-3's matrix multiplication and inversion
options let you solve problems relating to market
share, projecting receivable aging, inventory control, and other modeling problems for the natural
and social sciences. However, the specifics of
these applications and the theory behind matrix
operations are beyond the scope of this volume.

Options: The /Data Matrix command provides options for two algebraic matrix operations: multiplication and inversion.

Multiply: This option multiplies the individual components of two matrices according to the rules for matrix arithmetic. It assumes that only two matrices will be multiplied and that the number of columns in one matrix will be equal to the number of rows in a second matrix.

When you choose the Multiply option, 1-2-3 will prompt you for the location of the two matrix ranges. You can choose to type the cell addresses, reference the matrices with range names, or use the pointing method for specifying the ranges. When prompted for the output range, you can choose to enter the complete range or a reference to it or just enter the upper left cell.

Invert: This option inverts any square matrix according to the rules for matrix algebra. 1-2-3 will prompt you for the range of the matrix to invert and the output range. When prompted for the output range, you can enter the complete range or a reference to it or just enter the upper left cell.

Note: Addition and subtraction on matrices can be handled with the /File Combine Add and /File Combine Subtract options.

▶ /Data Parse

Description: The /Data Parse command is new in Release 2. It creates individual field values from the long labels stored in worksheet cells. You will need to use this command after you have used /File Import to bring long labels from text files created by your word processor or other program into a column of cells. Unless you use the /Data Parse command, this column of long labels is limited to descriptive use or a string formula. Once the /Data Parse command is used to split the long labels into individual fields, however, you can use the results in numeric formulas and graphs.

Assuming some consistency in the format of the labels, /Data Parse can divide each label into a row of individual values, including label, value, date, and time entries. 1-2-3 will make a suggestion for splitting the label into its individual components, but you have the option of changing this recommendation.

Options: When you enter /Data Parse, 1-2-3 presents a submenu of the following six choices.

Format-Line: This is the most important option in the /Data Parse command. It determines how 1-2-3 will split the long labels into individual cell entries. You can use it to create a new format line or edit an existing one.

Creating a Format Line: Selecting the Create option under Format-Line will create a format line above the cursor location at the time you make the selection. Position your cursor one cell above the first long label in your column to be parsed before entering /Data Parse Format-Line Create. This will ensure that the format line is positioned correctly.

1-2-3 will place letters and special symbols in the format line to present its interpretation of how best to split the long label. The following letters and symbols are used:

D	-The first character of a date block.
L	-The first character of a label block.
S	-The character below should be skipped during the parse operation. This character is never generated by 1-2-3, but you can enter it manually through the Edit option.
T	-The first character of a time block.
V	-The first character of a value block.
>	-The block started by the letter that precedes it is continued. The entry that began with the letter will continue to be placed in one worksheet cell until a skip or another letter is encountered.
*	-A blank space immediately below the character. This position can become part of the previous block.

Editing a Format Line: After you have 1-2-3 create a format line, you can use the Edit option to make changes in it if you wish.

Input-Column: This is the location for the column of long labels imported from an ASCII text file. The range you specify should include the Format line.

Output-Range: This is the location that you want to use for the individual entries generated from the long labels. You have an option: You can enter the upper left cell in an area of the worksheet large enough for the output, or you can enter the complete range for the area. Each approach offers a different advantage. If you specify the complete range and it is not large enough, 1-2-3 will give you an error message rather than expand the range. This prevents data stored near the output range from being destroyed if additional space is needed. If you specify only the upper left cell of the output range, 1-2-3 will determine how much space is required, and if it needs the space it will write over cells containing entries.

Reset: This option eliminates the format line if you have generated it, along with any settings for input or output area, so that you can start over.

Go: The Go option tells 1-2-3 that you have

created and verified the accuracy of the format line and have defined the location of the input and output areas. It causes the long labels to be parsed according to the specifications given.

Quit: This option tells 1-2-3 that you have finished with /Data Parse and want to be returned to READY mode. You will have to either make this selection or press ESC to get rid of the /Data Parse menu.

▶ /Data Query Criterion

Description: The /Data Query Criterion command lets you specify the location of the criteria you have entered on the worksheet for data-base record selection. Criteria must already be entered on the worksheet when you issue this command.

Options: The only option you have with this command is which method you use to specify the criteria range. Pointing, keying the cell addresses, and using a range name are all acceptable methods of specifying the range.

▶ /Data Query Delete

Description: The /Data Query Delete command searches data-base records for specified criteria and deletes all the records in the input area that match the criteria. The data-base records must first be specified with /Data Query Input, and the criteria must be entered on the worksheet and specified with /Data Query Criterion.

Options: None.

Note: Since deleting eliminates data permanently, save your file before deleting records. This way you can always retrieve the file if you make a mistake in specifying your criteria and delete too many records. Another protective strategy is to use your criteria to extract records before you use the same criteria to delete information.

▶ /Data Query Extract

Description: The /Data Query Extract command searches data-base records for specified criteria and writes all the records from the input area that match the criteria to an output area on the worksheet. Before using this command, you must complete the following preliminary steps:

(1) Specify the data-base records to be searched with /Data Query Input; (2) enter the criteria for extraction on the worksheet and specify with /Data Query Criterion; and (3) specify an output area with /Data Query Output. This area must be large enough to hold all the extracted records and must be out of the way of your other data.

Options: None.

/Data Query Find

Description: The /Data Query Find command searches data-base records for specified criteria and individually highlights all the records from the input area that match those criteria. Before using this command, you must specify the data-base records to be searched with /Data Query Input. You must also enter the search criteria on the worksheet and specify them with /Data Query Criterion.

Options: None.

/Data Query Input

Description: The /Data Query Input command permits you to specify the location of the data-base you have entered on the worksheet. Data-base records should already be entered on the worksheet when you issue this command.

Options: The only option you have with this command is what method you use to specify the input range. Pointing, keying the cell addresses, and using a range name are all acceptable methods of specifying the range.

Note: The input range should always include the field names at the top of your data base.

▶ /Data Query Output

Description: The /Data Query Output command permits you to specify the location of the extract area you plan to use when pulling information from a data base. The field names for the data you wish to extract should already be entered on the worksheet when you issue this command.

Options: You have two options with this command: you can specify the entire output area, or you can specify just the top row. You also have a number of options for specifying the range for the output area.

If you specify a one-row output range that includes only the field names, 1-2-3 will use as many rows as required for writing data in the columns selected for the output range. If you specify a multiple-row output range, 1-2-3 will stop extracting records when your output range is full. Options for specifying the range are pointing, keying the cell addresses, and using a range name.

▶ /Data Query Quit

Description: This command permits you to exit the sticky Data Query menu.

Options: None.

▶ /Data Query Reset

Description: This command will clear the range specifications for Input, Criterion, and Output.

Options: None.

▶ Data Query Unique

Description: The /Data Query Unique command searches data-base records for specified criteria and writes all the nonduplicate records from the input area that match the criteria to an output area on the worksheet. Before using this command, you must complete the following preliminary steps:

(1) Specify the data-base records to be searched with /Data Query Input; (2) enter the criteria for search on the worksheet and specify with /Data Query Criterion; and (3) specify an output area with /Data Query Output. This area must be large enough to hold all the selected records and must be out of the way of your other data.

Options: None.

▶ /Data Regression

Description: The / Data Regression command was added to Release 2 to let you perform a statistical analysis to see whether two or more variables are interrelated. This command allows you to use from 1 to 16 independent variables for your regression analysis. It will estimate the accuracy with which these independent variables can predict the values of a specified dependent variable.

For example, suppose that your dependent variable is the sales of hot chocolate at a football concession stand. You may wish to look at outdoor temperature and pregame ticket sales as possible predictors of how many cups of hot chocolate will be sold at a game. These two factors, outdoor temperature and pregame ticket sales, would be your independent variables. By applying regression analysis to historic data for the three variables, you could determine how effective the independent variables are as predictors of the dependent variable. When the regression analysis has been completed, 1-2-3 will display the number of observations, the Y intercept or constant, the standard error of estimated Y values and X coefficients, R squared, the X coefficients, and the degrees of freedom.

As with many of the other data commands, / Data Regression involves a few preliminary steps. First, you must place your dependent and independent variable values in columns on the worksheet. Each column should have the same number of entries, and all of them should contain numeric values. You can have a maximum of 8192 values with Release 2 and 2048 values with Release 1A, one value for each row of the worksheet. Second, you need to choose a blank area of the worksheet for 1-2-3 to use for output. This area must be at least nine rows in length and four columns wide. The width will need to exceed the number of independent variables by two. After you have completed these preliminary steps, you will need to use several of the /Data Regression options to complete your analysis.

Options: The /Data Regression submenu has seven options, as follows.

X-Range: This is the column or columns (16 maximum) that contain the values for your independent variables. X-Range can be specified by entering cell addresses or a range name or by pointing with your cursor to highlight the selected area.

Y-Range: This is the column containing the values for your dependent variable. You can specify it as a range name or cell addresses, or by pointing.

Output-Range: This is the area that will contain the results of the analysis. It must be at least nine rows deep and four columns wide, and it must be at least two columns wider than the number of independent variables you are using. You have the option of specifying the entire range or just the upper left corner. If you use the latter approach, 1-2-3 will decide the size of the area to use for the output of the regression analysis. Any data within cells of the output range will be overwritten.

Intercept: This is the Y intercept. You have the option of having 1-2-3 compute this value or setting it to zero. Compute is the default setting.

Reset: This option eliminates all the settings you have established for /Data Regression.

Go: This option completes the regression analysis after you have chosen X-Range, Y-Range, Output-Range, and Intercept.

Quit: This option exits the /Data Regression menu and returns you to READY mode.

▶ /Data Sort Data-Range

Description: The /Data Sort Data-Range command permits you to specify the location of the records you plan to sort. Data-base records should already be entered on the worksheet when you issue this command.

Options: The only option you have with this command is which method you use to specify the input range. Pointing, keying the cell addresses, and using a range name are all acceptable methods of specifying the range.

Note: The sort range should not include the field names at the top of the data base. If you accidentally include the field names, 1-2-3 will sort them.

▶ /Data Sort Go

Description: The /Data Sort Go command tells 1-2-3 that it is time to sort the records. Before this command is executed, you need to define the data base with the /Data Sort Data-Range command. In addition, specify the primary key and, potentially, the secondary key.

Options: None.

▶ /Data Sort Primary-Key

Description: The /Data Sort Primary-Key command permits you to specify a new sequence for your data-base records by selecting a field to control the resequencing. Enter the address of a data-containing cell within the field that you wish to use for controlling the sort sequence.

Options: The command lets you specify either ascending or descending sort order.

▶ /Data Sort Quit

Description: The /Data Sort Quit option is used to exit the sticky Sort menu.

Options: None.

▶ /Data Sort Reset

Description: The /Data Sort Reset command cancels the current settings for the primary and secondary keys and the data range.

Options: None.

▶ /Data Sort Secondary-Key

Description: The /Data Sort Secondary Key command lets you select a field within the data base to serve as a tie breaker in case there is more than one primary key with the same value. When this situation occurs, Sort uses the secondary key to provide a sequence for the records containing the duplicate entries. For example, if you have an employee file, you may choose the last-name field as the primary key and the first-name field as the secondary key. Then, if you encounter three employees with the last name of Smith, the three Smiths will appear in a sequence determined by their first names.

You select a secondary key the same as you do a primary key. Any data-containing cell within a field can be specified as the secondary key.

Options: You have two options for this command: A for ascending and D for descending sort order.

▶ /Data Table 1

Description: The /Data Table 1 command allows you to use different values of a variable in formulas. This command provides a structured what-if feature that substitutes various values in your formulas and records the result of each value.

The /Data Table 1 command builds what is called a one-way table. The table will have one set of input values running down its left side. It can evaluate many formulas.

The /Data Table 1 command requires that you set up a table area in your worksheet. The purpose of the table is to structure the input values that you would like to plug into an input cell one by one, while recording the impact of these values on the formulas that are also part of the table. To set up the table, place the input values you wish to use in a column in a blank area of your worksheet. The formulas you wish to have evaluated should begin one row above the first value and one column to the right. You may place new formulas in these cells, or you may reference other cells in the worksheet that contain the desired formulas. For example, to have a formula in A3 evaluated, you would place +A3 in one of the cells in this formula row. You may also wish to format the formula cells as text for documentation purposes. The two sets of entries just discussed will create the framework for the table. The value cells form the left edge of the table, with the last entry determining the bottom edge of the table. The row of formulas forms the top of the table, with the last entry in the row marking the right edge.

After the initial setup, you are ready to respond to 1-2-3's prompts to define the location of your table and the cell you wish to reference for input.

Options: After you have entered / Data Table 1, you will need to tell 1-2-3 the location you have selected for the table. The best method is to position your cursor at the upper left edge of the table before you enter the command. The table should be a rectangular area that includes all the formulas and all the values you are concerned with. To communicate the table location, you can use cell addresses, a range name, or the pointing method.

Next, 1-2-3 will ask you what worksheet cell you want to use as an input cell. This is the cell into which 1-2-3 will place the values in the table column one by one. Using a given value for the input cell, 1-2-3 will evaluate each of the table formulas and place the result of the formula in the column beneath the formula on the row for the input value being used. When 1-2-3 has used each of your values, the table will be filled in with the formula results. Depending on the size of your table, this process may take up to several minutes. When 1-2-3 has completed the table, the input cell will still have its original value; 1-2-3 makes its substitutions behind the scenes without affecting the cell entry. A change to a value in the input table will not cause the table to recalculate. To get recalculation, you must reuse /Data Table. If you wish to reset the table location and input cell before using the command again, you can use /Data Table Reset to eliminate your previous settings.

▷ /Data Table 2

Description: The /Data Table 2 command allows you to pick any two cells on the worksheet that contain numeric variable values and set up substitution values for these cells. This procedure lets you measure the impact of the changes in the result of a particular worksheet formula. This feature provides a structured approach to "what-if" analysis, in which 1-2-3 does most of the work.

The /Data Table 2 command produces a table

that is similar to a one-way table, except that you can substitute values for two variables at once and can evaluate only one formula. It allows you to see whether the formula result is more sensitive to changes in variable one or variable two, which provides an easy-to-use sensitivity analysis feature.

The / Data Table 2 command requires that you set up a table area in your worksheet. The purpose of the table is to structure values that you would like to plug into the two input cells, one by one, while recording the impact of these values on the result of a formula that is also part of the table. To set up the table, place the input values for the first variable you wish to use in a column in a blank area of your worksheet. The values for the second input cell you wish to use should begin one row above the first value and one column to the right. Place the values for this second variable across the row. You can use the / Data Fill command to supply these values if the increment between values is evenly spaced. Place the formula you wish to have evaluated for each value of the input variable in the blank cell at the intersection of the row and column of variable values. You may enter either an actual formula or a reference to a worksheet cell containing a formula. For example, to have a formula in A3 evaluated, you would place +A3 in the formula cell. You may also wish to format the formula cell as text for documentation purposes.

The two sets of entries just discussed will create the framework for the table, with the last entry determining the bottom edge. The row of value entries forms the top of the table, with the last entry in the row marking the right edge. To have 1-2-3 complete the table entries for you, enter /Data Table 2 and respond to 1-2-3's requests for specifications.

Options: After you have entered /Data Table 2, you will need to tell 1-2-3 the location you have selected for the table. To facilitate this process, position your cursor at the upper left edge of the table before entering /Data Table 2. The table should be a rectangular area that includes the formula and all the values you are concerned with. You can use cell addresses, a range name, or the pointing method to communicate the table location.

Next, 1-2-3 will ask you what worksheet cell you want to use as an input cell for the column of values you entered. This is the cell into which 1-2-3 will place the values in the table column, one by one. 1-2-3 will then ask what input cell will be used for the row of values. 1-2-3 will evaluate the formula shown at the upper left corner of the table, using each of the possible value combinations for input cell 1 and input cell 2.

When 1-2-3 has used each of your values, the table will be filled in with the formula results. Depending on the size of your completed table, this may take up to several minutes. When 1-2-3 has completed the table, the input cell will still have its original value, since 1-2-3 alters the values of the input cell only internally. A change to a value in the input table will not cause the table to recalculate. To get recalculation, you must reuse /Data Table. If you wish to reset the table location and input cell before using the command again, you can use /Data Table Reset to eliminate your previous settings.

▶ /Data Table Reset

Description: The /Data Table Reset command eliminates the settings you have established for the table location and input cell. Since 1-2-3 will suggest the previous setting the next time you use the command, Reset can be a convenience when the next table location or input-cell setting is far removed from the last use. If you select /Data Table before canceling your previous settings, you will have to press ESC and move your cursor to the new location in order to establish new settings. Once Reset is used, your cursor will remain in its current location.

▶ /File Combine Add

Description: The /File Combine Add command permits you to add some or all of the values from a worksheet file to current worksheet values. The addition process uses the cursor location in the current worksheet as the left uppermost cell to be combined with the first cell in the worksheet or range you are adding to it. Only cells that are blank or contain values will be affected by this process; cells that contain formulas or labels will not be affected.

The Add feature is useful when you are performing a budget consolidation. You can begin with a total budget worksheet that contains nothing more than labels and a few total formulas. As long as all departmental budgets are in exactly the same format as the total worksheet, you will be able to use /File Combine Add once for each worksheet file to produce a budget consolidation.

Options: Like the other /File Combine commands, Add permits you to combine an entire file or a named range. In either case, it begins the combination at the cursor location.

Entire-File: With this option, every value cell in the worksheet file will be added to a cell in the current worksheet. Cell A1 in the worksheet file will be added to the cell where the cursor rests in the current worksheet. Remaining values will be added to the cell with the proper displacement from the current cursor location.

When you select Entire-File, the names of the

worksheet files on the current disk (in the current directory if you are using a hard disk) will be presented. You can either point to one of the entries in the list of file names or you can enter the file name you wish to use. Since Release 2 lets you create file names that have a suffix different from the regular Release 2 suffix of .WK1, as long as you supply the proper suffix you can type the name of a file that has a suffix other than .WK1. Likewise, if you supply the complete pathname you can access files on a different drive or in a different directory.

Named-Range: With this option, 1-2-3 will ask you to specify a range name and then the file that contains this range name. You must specify a valid range name for the file name specified. The rules for entering the file name are the same as for Entire-File.

▶ /File Combine Copy

Description: The /File Combine Copy command permits you to replace some or all of the values from the current worksheet with values (including formulas and labels) from a worksheet file. The copying process uses the cursor location in the current worksheet as the upper leftmost cell you wish to replace with the first cell in the worksheet or range you are copying to it. Unlike the case with Add, even current worksheet cells containing formulas and labels are affected by /File Combine Copy. They will be overwritten by the copied information.

The Copy feature is useful when you want to copy headings and values from an existing worksheet to one you are currently creating. Although formulas can be copied, make sure that the values they will require are copied as well, or an error could result.

Options: Like the other /File Combine commands, Copy permits you to combine an entire file or a named range. In either case, it begins the replacement at the cursor location.

Entire-File: With this option, every value cell in the worksheet file will be added to a cell in the current worksheet. Cell A1 in the worksheet file will be added to the cell where the cursor rests in the current worksheet. Remaining values will be added to the cell with the proper displacement from the current cursor location.

When you select Entire-File, the names of the worksheet files on the current disk (or current directory, if you are using a hard disk) will be presented. You can either point to one of the entries in the list of file names or enter the file name you wish to use. Since Release 2 lets you create file names that have a suffix different from the regular Release 2 suffix of .WK1, as long as you supply the proper suffix you can type the name of a file that has a suffix other than .WK1. Likewise, if you supply the complete pathname you can access files on a different drive or different directory.

Named-Range: With this option, 1-2-3 will ask you to specify a range name and then the file that contains this range name. You must specify a valid range name for the file name specified. The rules for entering the file name are the same as for Entire-File.

▶ /File Combine Subtract

Description: The /File Combine Subtract command permits you to subtract some or all of the values from a worksheet file from the current worksheet values. The subtraction process uses the cursor location in the current worksheet as the upper leftmost cell to be combined with the first cell in the worksheet or range you are subtracting from it. Only cells that are blank or contain values will be affected by this process; cells that contain formulas or labels will not be affected.

The Subtract feature is useful when you are performing a budget consolidation. You can begin with a total budget worksheet. Then, to see the effect of closing one of a company's departments or subsidiaries, you can subtract the file containing its budget projections from the total. However, all subsidiary budgets must be in exactly the same format as the total worksheet.

Options: Like the other / File Combine commands, Subtract permits you to combine an entire file or a named range. In either case, it begins the combination at the cursor location.

Entire-File: With this option, every value cell in the worksheet file will be subtracted from a cell in the current worksheet. Cell A1 in the worksheet file will be subtracted from the cell where the cursor rests in the current worksheet. Remaining values will be subtracted from the cell with the proper displacement from the current cursor location.

When you select Entire-File, the names of the worksheet files on the current disk (or the current directory, if you are using a hard disk) will be presented. You can either point to one of the entries in the list of file names or enter the file name you wish to use. Since Release 2 allows you to create file names that have a suffix different from the regular Release 2 suffix of .WK1, as long as you supply the proper suffix, you can type the name of a file that has a suffix other than .WK1. Likewise, if you supply the complete pathname you can access files on a different drive or different directory.

Named-Range: With this option, 1-2-3 will ask you to specify a range name and then the file that contains this range name. The range name you specify must be a valid name for the file name specified. The rules for entering the file name are the same as for Entire-File.

▶ /File Directory

Description: The /File Directory command allows you to check or change the current root directory that 1-2-3 is using for file storage and retrieval. Under Release 2, the default directory is drive A; under Release 1A, it is drive B. This original default is stored in the file 123.CNF, which 1-2-3 checks every time you load 1-2-3 into your system. The /File Directory command allows you to make a change only for the current session. If you wish to change the default directory permanently, use /Worksheet Global Default Directory, followed by /Worksheet Global Default Update to save your change.

Options: With this command, you have the choice of reviewing the current directory setting or making a change to it. To review the setting, simply press ENTER in response to the display you see when you type /File Directory.

To make a change to the directory, you must first decide whether you want to change the complete directory designated or whether you want to stay in the same directory and just change the lower-level subdirectory you are working in. You can use this command to change the drive, the directory, and the subdirectory.

Drive: To change the drive, type the drive designator followed by a backslash; for example, B:\. To change the path as well, type the pathname at the same time; for example, B:\123SALES.

Current Directory: If the current directory is ACCT and you want to change it to MKTG, enter MKTG\.

A Lower Level in the Current Directory: This allows you to maintain the current directory setting but use a specific subdirectory within it. If your current directory is C:123\SALES and you wish to be in the subdirectory MICHIGAN within SALES, enter \MICHIGAN or C:123\SALES\MICHIGAN.

A Higher Level in the Current Directory: To change the directory to one level higher, enter .. (this is the DOS symbol for a directory one level higher). If your current directory level is C:123\SALES\MICHIGAN and you want to be at the level of SALES, you can enter either C:123\SALES or .. (the latter is clearly much quicker).

Note: When you use Release 1A with Release 1.1 of DOS, subdirectories are not allowed.

▶ /File Erase

Description: The /File Erase command is used to remove one or more files from the disk.

Options: You must first choose the type of the file or files you wish to remove from the disk. With Release 2, you have the following options: (1) Worksheet Files with the suffix .WK1; (2) Print Files with the suffix .PRN; (3) Graph Files with the suffix .PIC; and (4) Other Files with a suffix other than .WK1, .PRN, or .PIC.

With Release 1A, only the first three options are possible, and worksheet files have the suffix .WKS.

Once you have specified the file type you wish to delete, 1-2-3 will list all the files of that type on the current drive or directory. You can point to the file you wish to delete or you can type in the file name. If the file you wish to delete is on a different file or in a different directory, you will have to type the drive designator and pathname in addition to the file name (Release 2 only; with Release 1A, you will need to use /File Directory first).

You can use wildcard characters when specifying the file names you wish to delete. The special characters used in creating wildcard file names are as follows:

?   Will match any single character in the
file name. For example, ?CCT would
match ACCT, TCCT, and LCCT.

*   Matches all remaining characters in
the file name. For example, S*matches
SALES, SALES1, and SALARY.

▶ /File Import

Description: The /File Import command permits
you to load information in a Print file into the
current worksheet at the cursor location. Standard ASCII files that do not exceed 240 characters
in width and 8192 characters in length (2048 lines
for Release 1A) can be imported, as long as each
file has a suffix of .PRN.

Options: The /File Import command provides two
options, allowing you to bring either a column of
long labels or a combination of numbers and labels into the worksheet.

Text: This option will bring each line of the
imported text file into the worksheet as a single
long label. /Data Parse can split files imported as
text into separate entries rather than one long
label.

Numbers: This option searches the imported file
for numbers and for text entries enclosed in
quotes. Each number will be placed in a work-

sheet cell as a value, and each entry in quotes will be placed in the worksheet cell as a left justified label. If more than one number or quote-enclosed entry is found in a line of the text file, more than one column of the worksheet will be used. When the next line of the imported file is processed, entries will again begin in the same column as the cursor.

Note: Special characters added by some word processors can cause problems. Most word processors have an option that excludes these special characters to produce a standard ASCII file.

▶ /File List

Description: The /File List command lists all the files of the specified type in the current directory.

Options: With Release 2, you have four choices: (1) Worksheet Files with the suffix .WK1; (2) Print Files with the suffix .PRN; (3) Graph Files with the suffix .PIC; and (4) Other Files with a suffix other than .WK1, .PRN, or .PIC.

With Release 1A, only the first three options are possible. Also with Release 1A, worksheet files have the suffix .WKS.

▶ /File Retrieve

Description: The /File Retrieve command loads a

file from disk into the memory of your computer system. Any information in memory before the file is retrieved is erased by the loading of the new file.

Options: You can retrieve a file from the current disk or directory, or you can retrieve from a different one if you specify the pathname (Release 2 only; with Release 1A, you must change directories with /File Directory first). With Release 2, you can retrieve password-protected files by supplying the password when 1-2-3 prompts you.

▶ /File Save

Description: The /File Save command allows you to save the current worksheet, and any settings you have created for it, to a worksheet file.

Options: You can save the worksheet file to the current disk by entering the file name and pressing ENTER if the file has never been saved to the disk. Under Release 2, if you wish to use a different disk or directory than the current one, you can do so by specifying the complete pathname. With Release 1A, you must use /File Directory.

If the file is already saved on the disk, 1-2-3 will prompt you with the existing file name. Press ENTER to accept it. The next prompt is Cancel or Replace. Cancel stops the /File Save command and returns you to READY mode. Replace places the current contents of memory on the disk under the existing file name, replacing what was stored in the file previously.

This command also allows you to add a password to a file when it is saved. Once a file is saved with a password, you will not be able to retrieve the file unless you can supply the password. After typing the name of the file to be saved, press the space bar and type p. This causes 1-2-3 to prompt you for a password up to 15 characters long. After you enter one, a verify prompt will ask for you to type the password again. If you wish to abort the procedure instead of responding to the verify prompt, you can press ESCAPE several times to return to READY mode without saving the file and adding a password.

Note: If you save a file with the name AUTO123, the file will be retrieved every time you load 1-2-3, as long as it is in the same directory as 1-2-3.

▶ /File Xtract

Description: The /File Xtract command allows you to save a portion of the current worksheet in a worksheet file. Settings established for the current worksheet, such as graph and print settings and range names, are saved in the new file.

Options: The /File Xtract command allows you to

save either values or formulas from the range specified.

Formulas: This option saves current worksheet formulas, as well as labels and values, in the worksheet file.

Values: This option saves numbers and labels in the worksheet files. Formulas are evaluated to determine the numbers for saving, but the formulas are not saved.

After entering the /File Xtract command and choosing Formulas or Values, select a file name for saving from the menu or enter a new name. Next, enter a range of cell addresses or a range name. If the file name is new, press ENTER to complete the process. If you are using an existing file name, 1-2-3 will present you with a prompt asking if you wish to Cancel the request or Replace the existing file with the contents of the range selected.

Note: You can use /File Combine to add this extracted information to a worksheet file in memory.

▶ /Graph A B C D E F

Description: This is actually six different commands. Each assigns one data range to be displayed on a graph. For example, you could enter

/Graph A and then specify your first data range by entering the range, pointing to the range, or entering a range name.

Options: These commands allow you to use from one to six data ranges. To use six data ranges, enter each of the letter codes from A through F individually and reference the data you want assigned to each one. If you are using only one data range (in a pie chart, for example), specify it with option A.

▶ /Graph Name Create

Description: The /Graph Name Create command assigns a name to the current set of graph settings and stores them with your worksheet. If you want this name and its settings available during your next 1-2-3 session, be sure to save the worksheet with /File Save.

Options: Your only option for this command is the name you select. The name follows the rules for range names rather than file names. You can use up to 15 characters for the name.

Note: If you select a name that has already been assigned to another graph, 1-2-3 will not warn you. Instead, it will overwrite the existing settings with the current settings without asking you.

/Graph Name Delete

Description: The /Graph Name Delete command removes unneeded graph names from the worksheet individually. Since this process frees up some memory space, it is useful to purge graph names and their associated settings with this command when you no longer need them.

Options: None.

/Graph Name Reset

Description: This command removes all graph names and their settings from the worksheet. Since there is no prompt before the actual deletion, you risk losing all your graph definitions if you accidentally choose Reset from the Graph Name menu.

Options: None.

/Graph Name Use

Description: The /Graph Name Use command allows you to choose a graph name from the list associated with the current worksheet. The graph whose name is selected will become the current graph. You can either type the graph name or point to it in the list that 1-2-3 displays.

▶ /Graph Options B&W

Description: This command displays graphs in one color. To differentiate between a group of bars on a bar chart, 1-2-3 will automatically add hatch-mark patterns when the B&W option is in effect. You can choose to use hatch-mark patterns for a pie chart by adding the codes for the patterns you wish to use. The codes should be placed on the worksheet and referenced as the B data range.

Options: None.

▶ /Graph Options Color

Description: This command displays your graphs in color.

Options: None.

Note: Never save a graph for which you have chosen Color to be printed unless you have a color printer or plan to use a plotter. If you choose Color and have a standard printer, you will not get the hatch-mark patterns that differentiate between parts of pie charts and bar graphs when you choose B&W.

▶ /Graph Options Data-Labels

Description: The /Graph Options Data-Labels command permits you to add specific labels to a range of data points. 1-2-3 will obtain these data labels from the range of worksheet cells you specify.

Options: You can choose where to place the data labels in relation to your data points. Your options are Center, Above, Left, Right, and Below.

Note: With a line graph, you can use data labels as the only markers for your data points. To do this, choose /Graph Options Format Neither to remove lines and symbols.

▶ /Graph Options Format

Description: The /Graph Options Format command allows you to select the type of line or XY graph you will create. This command will determine whether data points are shown as symbols, are connected with a line, or are marked with both symbols and a line (or neither).

Options: Your first choice is the range that the format will apply to. You can specify Graph as the range if you want your selection used for all ranges on the graph, or you can select a specific data range by entering a letter from A through F.

After selecting the range for the format, you have the choice of specifying Lines, Symbols, Both, or Neither. Choosing Lines will show the data points connected by a line, on which the data points are not marked. Symbols will show only symbols, with no connecting line. (1-2-3 uses a different symbol for each of the ranges.) A choice of Both will show both the symbols and a connecting line. A choice of Neither shows neither lines nor symbols. It is useful in conjunction with the Data-Labels option when you center a data label on a point to mark it and do not want any other marking on the graph.

▶ /Graph Options Grid

Description: The /Graph Options Grid command will add vertical lines, horizontal lines, or both to a graph. These lines start at the markers on the X or Y axis and extend upward or to the right, depending on whether you choose Vertical, Horizontal, or Both. The lines can greatly aid in the interpretation of points on the graph.

Options: The options for /Graph Options Grid determine whether the grid lines are generated in one or both directions. The choices are as follows:

Horizontal: This option adds horizontal lines that extend across from the Y axis. These lines are effective with bar graphs, since they help you interpret the value for the top of each bar.

Vertical: This option adds vertical lines, which start at the X axis and extend upward. They are most effective with an XY or line graph; they tend to detract from the clarity of a bar graph.

Both: This option adds lines in both directions at once. The lines form a grid pattern on the graph.

Clear: This option eliminates grid lines that you have added to a graph.

▶ /Graph Options Legend

Description: This command displays legends at the bottom of your graph that describe the data represented by the different data ranges.

Options: You can choose any one of the ranges from A through F each time you request this command. You can either enter a legend of up to 19 characters or reference a cell address containing the legend you wish to use. If you use the latter approach, the legend may exceed 19 characters.

Note: If you use a cell reference for the legend and

later move this cell on the worksheet, 1-2-3 will
not adjust the legend reference. You can eliminate
this problem by using a range name for the referenced cell.

▶ /Graph Options Scale Skip

Description: This command permits you to
remove the congestion and overlap that can
occur when you assign labels to be displayed
along the X axis. The skip factor you specify will
let you use only some of the labels in the range. If
you specify a skip factor of 3, for example, only
every third label will be used.

Options: You can specify any number from 1 to
8191 for the skip factor. The default is 1, meaning
that 1-2-3 uses every label in the range.

▶ /Graph Options Scale X-Scale

Description: This command permits you to let 1-2-
3 choose the scale for the X axis or, alternatively,
to choose the scale yourself.

Options: There are seven options for the /Graph
Options Scale X-Scale command.

Automatic: This setting is the default. It lets 1-2-
3 determine the proper scale.

Manual: This option informs 1-2-3 that you want to determine the scale range.

Lower: This is the lower limit or the smallest value that can be shown on your scale. You define it when you select Manual.

Upper: This is the upper limit or the highest value that can be shown on your scale. You define it when you select Manual.

Format: This option allows you to select a display format (currency, percent, or the like) for the numeric values represented on the scale. Use it only for XY graphs.

Indicator: This option, available only in Release 2, permits you to turn off the display of the size indicator for the scale. The default is Yes, allowing 1-2-3 to display indicators such as thousands.

Quit: This option exits the command and returns you to the Graph Options menu.

▶ /Graph Options Scale Y-Scale

Description: This command permits you to let 1-2-3 choose the scale for the Y axis or, alternatively, to choose the scale yourself.

Options: There are seven options for the /Graph Options Scale Y-Scale command, as follows:

Automatic: This setting is the default. It lets 1-2-3 determine the proper scale.

Manual: This option informs 1-2-3 that you want to determine the scale range.

Lower: This is the lower limit or the smallest value that can be shown on your scale. You define it when you select Manual.

Upper: This is the upper limit or the highest value that can be shown on your scale. You define it when you select Manual.

Format: This option allows you to select a display format (currency, percent, or the like) for the numeric values represented on the scale.

Indicator: This option, available only in Release 2, permits you to turn off the display of the size indicator for the scale. The default is Yes, allowing 1-2-3 to display indicators like thousands.

Quit: This option exits the command and returns you to the Graph Options menu.

/Graph Options Titles

Description: This command permits you to add titles to your graph to improve its clarity and readability. Your titles will be limited to 39 characters if you enter them at the prompt for the command. If you use references to a worksheet cell instead, you can exceed the 39-character limit for all but the vertical option. To reference a stored title, you must enter a backslash (\) and a cell address containing the title.

Options: You can add titles at the top of your graph or along the axes with the options available. You have four choices:

First: The label you enter after this choice will be centered at the top of your graph.

Second: Your entry for this option will be centered and placed immediately below the label shown by the First option.

X-Axis: This option places a title below the X axis.

Y-Axis: This option places your entry vertically to the left of the Y axis.

Note: If you use a cell reference for the legend and move the referenced cell on the worksheet later on, 1-2-3 will not adjust the title reference. This problem can be eliminated by using a range name for the referenced cell.

/Graph Quit

Description: This command exits the Graph menu and returns you to the worksheet READY mode.

Options: None.

/Graph Reset

Description: The /Graph Reset command cancels the graph settings you selected previously.

Options: You can choose to cancel all or some of the graph settings with the options for this command. You have four choices:

Graph: This option cancels all graph settings.

X: This option cancels the X data values.

A-F: Choosing one of this set of options cancels the data range for the letter code selected.

Quit: This option tells 1-2-3 that you have canceled all the settings you wanted to eliminate and returns you to the previous menu.

▶ /Graph Save

Description: The / Graph Save command saves the current graph picture in a .PIC file. This file is separate from your worksheet. It can be used by the PrintGraph program but not by 1-2-3.

Options: After selecting this command, you have the choice of entering a file name or choosing one from the list that 1-2-3 presents. If you choose to use an existing .PIC file name, 1-2-3 will prompt you to determine whether you really want to reuse that file (and therefore overwrite it) or cancel your request.

▶ /Graph Type

Description: The / Graph Type command allows you to pick a format for displaying your data. You have five different graph formats to choose from. You can easily change from one to another without any alterations, other than selecting another type.

Options: This command provides five options, as follows:

Line: This choice plots the points of a data range and connects them with a line. The default is to use both symbols and a line on the graph. Symbols mark each point, and a line joins the data points. You can use the /Graph Options Format command to change the display so that it uses just a line or just symbols, if you prefer. You can generate up to six separate lines, displaying six data ranges, on one graph.

Bar: This uses up to six sets of vertical bars to represent the data ranges selected. 1-2-3 will use hatch-mark patterns to distinguish the different data ranges, unless you select /Graph Options Color and show the bars in different colors.

XY: This option pairs X range values with values from the A to F data ranges. You can use the /Graph Options Format command to connect the points with a line or display them as symbols. With this kind of graph, 1-2-3 generates a numeric scale for the X axis as well as the Y axis.

Stacked-Bar: For one data range, a stacked bar graph will appear the same as an ordinary bar graph. When additional data ranges are graphed, however, a difference is evident. Rather than adding the second set of bars to the right of the first, the stacked bar graph option stacks the second set on top of the first, the third on top of the second, and so on. The total height of a bar thus indicates the total of the values for that category. The different bars in a stack will be distinguished by hatch-mark patterns unless you choose /Graph Options Color.

Pie: A pie chart is used to show the size of each of several categories relative to the whole. Each category shown in the chart will be represented by a wedge whose size is proportional to its value in comparison with the values for the other categories shown in the chart. Only one set of data, the A range, can be shown. A B range can be used to indicate colors or hatch-mark patterns with a number code from 0 to 7. If 100 is added to the code in the B range, the piece of the pie represented by that code will be exploded (removed from the pie and shown as a separate slice).

▶ /Graph View

Description: The /Graph View command displays the graph that you have defined by selecting data ranges and a graph type. If you have not defined a graph, the screen will appear blank when you select this command. To return to the Graph menu when you are through with the View option, press ESC.

Options: None.

Note: If your 1-2-3 package is installed for a graphics device that is different from the one you are using, when you press View your screen will appear blank. To correct the problem, go back to the installation process for the 1-2-3. Similarly, if you attempt to use the package on a system without graphics support, entering /Graph View will cause the screen to appear blank. In both cases you can press ESC to return to the Graph menu.

▶ /Graph X

Description: The /Graph X command is used to label the points on the X axis for a line or bar graph. For a pie chart the X values provide labels for the pie segments, and for an XY chart they provide values to plot against the Y values. The labels assigned to the points must be stored in worksheet cells and specified. You can specify by using a range name or a range address, or by pointing to the cells you wish to use.

Options: None. If the labels you choose contain too many characters, they will overlap in the display, causing this area of the graph to be unreadable. You can use /Graph Options Scale Skip to tell 1-2-3 not to use every label.

▶ /Move

Description: The /Move command allows you to move a range of worksheet entries to any location on the worksheet. This command will adjust the formulas within the range to correspond to their new location if relative references (such as A3 or D4) are used. Absolute references within formulas (such as A2) will not be updated by the moving process.

Options: This command permits you to move one or many cells to a new location. For example, you can move A2 to B3 by entering /Move A2, pressing ENTER, then entering B3 and pressing ENTER. To move a range of cells to a new location, you might enter /Move A2..B6 and press ENTER, then enter a new destination, such as D2, and press ENTER. 1-2-3 will move the entire range, locating the contents of its left uppermost cell (A2) in the designated To cell. You can use any of the options for specifying ranges, such as pressing F3 (NAME), pointing to the range, or typing the complete range address.

▶ /Print File

Description: The /Print File command allows you to print a report to a disk file. This command is useful at times when your printer is not available. It can also be used to prepare data for other programs that manipulate 1-2-3's print output.

Options: All of the /Print Printer options are also valid when you choose /Print File. You will be able to select print ranges and apply any of the other options to them.

/Print Printer

Description: This command is used whenever you wish to print information from a worksheet file on your printer. Since the package contains default values for most of the Print parameters, printing can be as simple as specifying a print range. When you need greater sophistication or would like to tailor a report to your exact needs, you have a wide range of options to work with.

Options: The Printer command has the same options as the File command. You can make simple selections such as specifying the range of worksheet cells to print, or you can make more sophisticated selections such as specifying a set of printer control codes to meet your exact needs. You can change margins, select rows or columns to print on all pages of a report, print the worksheet cells as they display, or print the formulas behind them.

/Print Printer Align

Description: This command will set 1-2-3's internal line count to zero. 1-2-3 then assumes that the printer is aligned at the top of a page. Any entries after this point will begin to add to the new line count.

Options: There are no options for this command. Your only real concern is to make sure the printer carriage is stationed at the top of a form before you enter the command sequence.

▶ **/Print Printer Clear**

Description: This command can be used to eliminate some or all of the special print settings. It returns the specified print settings to the defaults. If you have added a setup string, header, footer, and borders when printing a report and want to print it again without these special features, the Clear option saves you time by eliminating these entries. Without it you would have to reexecute each of the commands for the special settings and delete the entries you had made.

Options: The four options for /Print Printer Clear let you decide whether you want to clear all or some print settings.

All: This option eliminates all the special entries made through the print menus. The current print range is canceled. Borders, headers, and footers are all eliminated. Margins, page length, and setup strings are returned to their default settings.

Range: This option cancels only the current print range.

Borders: This option clears both row and column borders.

Format: This option resets the margin, page length, and setup string to the default setting found under / Worksheet Global Default Printer.

/Print Printer Go

Description: This command tells 1-2-3 to begin transmitting the print range to the printer (if you selected Printer) or to your disk drive (if you selected File).

Options: None.

/Print Printer Line

Description: This command is used to generate a line feed. It allows you to print two ranges with only one line between them. This is done by selecting Line after printing the first range and then selecting the second range and printing it. It adds 1 to 1-2-3's internal line count.

Options: None.

Note: This command offers an advantage over the printer's line feed button, since the command increments 1-2-3's internal line count by one, keeping the printing of a page in sync with the page's physical length.

▶ /Print Printer Options

Description: This command provides access to all the bells and whistles 1-2-3 offers for printing. Through the submenu presented by this option, you can make many modifications to the appearance of a report.

Options: The Options menu includes choices for Header, Footer, Margins, Borders, Setup, Pg-Length, Other, and Quit. These options will be covered individually in the sections that follow.

▶ /Print Printer Options Borders

Description: The Borders option allows you to print specified rows or columns on every page. You select the option you wish (either rows or columns) and specify the range of cells you wish to have duplicated on each page. Be careful not to include the border rows or columns in your print range; otherwise they will be printed twice.

Options: With this command you have the choice of using either rows or columns as borders.

Rows: This is the option to use when you have a report that is too long for one page. To provide descriptive information on each page, select the border rows you wish to print again on the second and subsequent pages.

Columns: Use this option when your report is too wide for one sheet of paper and there is identifying information at the far left of your worksheet. The command will duplicate the selected column information at the left side of each page.

Note: If you accidentally select this command, the current row or column will become a border, depending on whether you choose Rows or Columns. To undo the damage, select / Print Printer Clear Borders.

▶ /Print Printer Options Footer

Description: This command allows you to add one line of up to 240 characters at the bottom of each page of a report. Typical contents for the line are date, report name or number, company name or department, and page number. 1-2-3 allows you to have three different entries for the footer line.

Options: The three Footer options let you place an entry at the left, center, or right section of the footer. Entries are separated by the vertical bar character. Use a bar to end each of the sections, even if they are not used (in other words, a single footer at the right should be preceded by two bars).

You also have the option of using @ or # in your footer. The # represents the current page number, and the @ represents the current date.

Note: If you include the page number in your footer, you will have to clear the Print options and respecify them before you print the report a second time. Otherwise, for the second printing 1-2-3 will pick up with the next page number rather than beginning again with page 1.

▶ /Print Printer Options Header

Description: This command allows you to add one line of up to 240 characters at the top of each page of a report. Typical contents for the line are date, report name or number, company name or department, and page number. 1-2-3 allows you to have three different entries for the header line.

Options: Header options allow you to place an entry at the left, center, or right section of the header. Entries are separated by the vertical bar character. Use a bar to end each of the sections, even if they are not used (in other words, a single header at the right should be preceded by two bars).

You also have the option of using @ or # in your header. The # represents the current page number, and the @ represents the current date.

Note: If you include the page number in your header, you will have to clear the Print options and respecify them before printing the report a second time. Otherwise, for the second printing 1-2-3 will pick up with the next page number rather than beginning again with page 1.

▶ /Print Printer Options Margins

Description: This command allows you to control the amount of blank space at the top, bottom, and sides of a printed page. If you do not make an entry for Margins, the default values will be used.

Options: There is a Margins option for each of the four areas where you can control the amount of blank space on a printed page.

Left: The default setting for the left margin is 4 spaces. To establish a new setting, you can enter any number from 0 to 240. Make sure that the value you enter for the left margin is less than the value entered for the right margin, since the difference between these two values determines how many characters will print in a line of your report.

Right: The default setting for the right margin is 76. You can enter any number between 0 and 240 to change this margin setting. Make sure that the value you enter for the right margin is greater than the value entered for the left margin, since the difference between these two values determines how many characters will print in a line of your report.

Top: The default setting for the top margin is 2. You can enter any number from 0 to 32 (Release 2) to change the value for this setting.

Bottom: The default setting for the bottom margin is 2. You can enter any number from 0 to 32 (Release 2) to change the value for this setting.

▶ /Print Printer Options Other

Description: This is an unusual command in that it provides two very different sets of features. First, it lets you decide whether output should be the information displayed in worksheet cells or the formulas behind the display. Second, this command lets you determine whether print or file output should be formatted or unformatted. The

Unformatted option is especially useful if you are attempting to take 1-2-3 data into another program, since it will strip off headers and other special formats.

Options: The Other command has four options, which form two pairs. The effect of each member of a pair is the opposite of the effect of the other.

As-Displayed: This is the default option. It causes your printout to match the screen display in the active window in terms of cell values, format, and width. If you want to change the display from your normal worksheet display, you could set up a second window, make width and formatting changes to this window, and print from there. After printing, you could clear the window.

Cell-Formulas: This option causes the formulas for cells, rather than their results, to be displayed. The formulas are shown one per line down the page.

Formatted: This option prints the output with all of your formatting options, such as headers, footers, and page breaks. This is normally the way you want your output to appear when you send it to a printer.

Unformatted: This option strips all the formatting from your data. In other words, information is written to the output device without page breaks, headers, or footers. This option is useful when you are writing the output to a file for use by another program or when you want the printer to ignore page breaks.

▶ /Print Printer Options Pg-Length

Description: This option determines the number of lines in a page of output. The default is 66, but 1-2-3 (Release 2) will accept entries from 10 to 100. (Actually, there are not 66 lines of printed output on a default page; top and bottom margins, headers, footers, and the two blank lines below the header and above the footer must be subtracted from the page length to determine the number of print lines.)

Options: The only options for this command are to enter a page length between 10 and 100 for Release 2 and between 20 and 100 for Release 1A.

▶ /Print Printer Options Quit

Description: This command allows you to exit from the Options menu. Since this menu stays around for you to make a series of selections, you need Quit to make an exit when you have completed your selections.

Options: None.

► /Print Printer Options Setup

Description: This command allows you to transmit control codes to your printer. These control codes let you use the special features the printer offers. These special features may include enlarged, compressed, emphasized, or boldface printing as well as different numbers of lines to be printed per inch.

Options: The options available for this command are dictated by the features your printer supports. A few of the options for the Epson MX100 printer and their respective setup strings include:

\015	Set compressed print
\018	Stop compressed print
\027G	Start boldface print
\027H	Stop boldface print

You can find the decimal codes you need for setup strings in your printer manual. When entering them into 1-2-3, precede each code with a backslash and a zero, as in the example.

► /Print Printer Page

Description: This command advances the paper to the top of the next form. This is done right from the keyboard as the command is entered; there is no need to touch the printer. /Print Printer Page prints a footer if you have specified one.

Options: None.

/Print Printer Quit

Description: This command is used to exit the Print menu and place you back in READY mode. Since the Print menu stays around while you make selections, you will need to use Quit to leave it. Even after printing, you will not return to READY mode until you have chosen Quit. Pressing the ESC key produces the same result.

Options: None.

/Print Printer Range

Description: This command determines how much of the worksheet will be printed. You can specify any valid range of cells, from one cell to the entire worksheet. 1-2-3 will decide how much of the range can be placed on one page, based on the margin and page length settings, and will carry the remainder of the range over to additional pages.

Options: The only option for this command is to

specify a range. The format used for ranges is cell address..cell address, where the cell addresses specified are at opposite corners of the range of cells to be printed. For example, if you wanted to print cells A1 through D10, you could specify the range as A1..D10, D10..A1, D1..A10, or A10..D1.

▶ **/Range Erase**

Description: The /Range Erase command elimi-nates entries you have made in worksheet cells. Without this command, your only options for removing a cell entry would be to make a new entry in the cell, edit the cell's contents, or use the space bar to replace the entry with blanks. None of these approaches leaves a label cell completely blank, however, since at minimum the cell would still contain a label indicator.

Options: There are no special options for this command. Your only choices are whether to spec-ify a single cell or many cells in the range, and whether to type the range reference or highlight the included cells by pointing.

Note: The /Range Erase command does not affect cell formats. A cell formatted as currency will still be formatted as currency after /Range Erase is used. To eliminate a format you can use /Range Format and a new format option, or use /Range Format Reset to return the range to the default setting. The /Range Erase command also does not affect protection or cell width. Protected cells cannot be erased when worksheet protection is enabled. In this situation, 1-2-3 will give you an error message instead of erasing the protected cells.

/Range Format

Description: The /Range Format command allows you to determine the appearance of numeric entries on your worksheet. With this command you can change the specific display format for one or many cells in a contiguous range on the worksheet. You will be able to choose the number of decimal places displayed (0 to 15) for most formats and determine whether the numeric information is displayed as currency, scientific notation, a date, a time (Release 2 only), or one of several other options.

The display format you select will not affect the internal storage of numbers. You can elect to display a number with seven decimal places as a whole number, for example, but all seven places will be maintained internally.

Regardless of the format you choose, the column must be wide enough to display your selection. If the column is not wide enough, *'s will appear. For example, if you used a column width of 3 and attempted to format a number as currency with two decimal places, a display of asterisks would result; the $ and the decimal point also take up space.

Options: There are 11 options for you to choose from. 1-2-3 provides a menu to let you define your format. To use the /Range Format command, enter /Range Format and select the option you wish to use. Then respond to 1-2-3's prompts concerning the number of decimal places (or the Date format) you desire. Finally, select the range of cells to be formatted, either by entering the address or a range name or by highlighting the cells with your cursor.

Fixed: Fixed format allows you to display all entries with a specific number of decimal places. Two places are the default, but you may select any number between 0 and 15. Examples with three decimal places are .007, 9.000, and 4.156.

Scientific: Scientific format displays numbers in exponential form, showing the power of 10 that the number must be multiplied by. This format allows you to concisely represent very large or very small numbers. From 0 to 15 places can be specified for the multiplier. Some examples with two decimal places are 6.78E-20, 4.11E+5, and 0.78E+8.

Currency: Currency format will cause your

entry to be preceded by a dollar sign ($). It will also insert a separator, such as a comma, between the thousands and hundreds positions. You may specify from 0 to 15 decimal places for this format; 2 is the default. Negative amounts will appear in parentheses. Examples with two decimal places are $3.40, $1,400.98, and ($89.95).

, (Comma): The Comma format is identical to the Currency format, except that Comma lacks the dollar sign ($). Comma format uses the thousands separator and allows you to specify any number of decimal places you want between 0 and 15. Two decimal places is the default. Negative numbers are displayed in parentheses. Examples with two decimal places are 1,200.00, (5,678.00), and 45.00.

General: General is the default format for 1-2-3. With this format, the leading zero integer will always appear, as in 0.78, but trailing zeros will be suppressed. If the number is very large or very small, it will appear in scientific notation. Examples of numeric displays with the General format are 15.674, 2.7E+12, and 0.67543.

+/−: This format produces a horizontal bar graph showing the relative size of numbers. Each integer is represented by a symbol. For example, −3 would be −−−, and 5 would be +++++. A . is used to represent 0.

Percent: Percent format displays your entries as percentages. Each entry will be multiplied by 100, and a % symbol will be added to the end. Because of this multiplication, you must enter percents as their decimal equivalent. For example, you must enter .05 for 5%. If you enter 5 and format the cell as Percent, it will display as 500%. You may specify from 0 to 15 decimal places; 2 is the default. Examples with two decimal places are 4.00%, 3.15%, and 1200.00%.

Date: The Date option is the only format choice that provides a second menu of possibilities. From this second menu you can select specific formats for the date. The following formats are accessible through the date option:

D1	(DD-MMM-YY)	08-Sep-86
D2	(DD-MMM)	08-Sep
D3	(MMM-YY)	Sep-86
D4	(MM/DD/YY)	09/08/86
D5	(MM/DD)	09/08

In Release 2, Time formats are accessed through the Date format. When you select Time from the Date options, a menu of four time formats will be presented. Two of the formats use the AM and PM designation, and the other two are international formats that use a 24-hour day, like military time. The formats available for the display of time in your worksheet cells can be seen in the following table.

(D6) T1 HH:MM:SS AM/PM   06:00:00 AM
(D7) T2 HH:MM AM/PM   06:00 AM
(D8) T3 Long International   06:00:00 *
(D9) T4 Short International   06:00 *

* This format can be changed to a number of options with the /Worksheet Global Default Other International command.

Text: Text format displays the cells selected exactly as you have entered them. In the case of formulas, the formula will be displayed, rather than the result.

Hidden: Hidden format causes the selected cells to appear blank on the screen. If you move your cursor to one of these cells, the control panel will display the entry you made in the cell.

Reset: This option returns the range of cells you select to the default format setting.

▶ /Range Input

Description: This command is used to restrict cursor movement to unprotected cells. To use the command, first construct a worksheet and make sure the desired input cells are unprotected with /Range Unprotect. Then enable worksheet protection with /Worksheet Global Protection Enable. Next, enter /Range Input and select a range of unprotected cells for the input area. Remember that ranges must be rectangular; this command will not work on input cells scattered across the entire worksheet.

Options: While in the /Range Input command you can use many of the cursor-movement keys to move among the unprotected cells in the selected area. HOME moves to the first unprotected cell, and END moves to the last cell. The arrow keys will move you within the selected range. ESC can be used to cancel an entry; however, if you have not made an entry, ESC will cancel /Range Input. ENTER can be used to finalize entries; however, if no entries have been made, ENTER will cancel /Range Input. Selections cannot be made from the command menus, although some of the function keys are operational. These keys are F1 (HELP), F2 (EDIT), and F9 (CALC).

Note: This command is especially useful in the macro environment where you are attempting to automate applications for inexperienced 1-2-3 users.

▶ /Range Justify

Description: The /Range Justify command lets you change the way a label is displayed. Once a label is entered (for instance, a long label entered in cell A1), you use /Range Justify to redistribute the

label so that it is displayed differently. For
instance, the long label in cell A1 might be displayed in the range A1..C3. The width of the
display is determined by selecting a justify range,
which may be one to several cells wide (the maximum is 240 characters) and one to several rows
long.

If you use /Range Justify to redistribute a
label in cell A1 to the single-row justify range
A1..C1, the label will be reformatted to display in
the first three columns of however many rows it
takes to display the full label. The label will be
contained only in the cells of column A, however.

Information in cells to the right of a justify
range is not displaced when you use /Range Justify. Instead, the display of a label in the justify
range is truncated, even though the contents of
the cells containing the label are not affected.

Options: You have the option of specifying one or
more rows for the justify range. If you specify
one row, 1-2-3 will include all labels from that
row down to either the bottom of the worksheet
or the first row that does not contain a label.
Cells containing nonlabel entries below the justify
range may be shifted up or down, depending on
the space requirements for the justified labels.

If you specify more than one row with /Range
Justify, you assume the burden of allowing sufficient space for the justification. If there is not
enough space in the range you choose, you will

see the error message "Justify range is full or line is too long." When you select more than one row for the range, only the labels in the range down to the first nonlabel entry will be justified. Also, when you specify more than one row, cells outside the justify range will be unaffected.

Note: Do not use this command for cells that have been assigned range names. Although the contents of the cell may be displaced, the range name will still be assigned to the same cell.

▶ /Range Label

Description: The /Range Label command is used to change the justification (placement) of existing worksheet labels. Cells within the range that are blank will not save the label indicator entered with /Range Label and apply it to later entries, however. These later entries will use the default worksheet setting.

Options: /Range Label has three options: Left, Center, and Right. These selections dictate the label indicator that will be used for existing cell entries. Using Left changes the label indicator to ' for all entries in the range and causes all the entries to be left justified in the cell. Using Center places a ^ at the front of each label and causes the existing labels to appear in the center of the cells.

The last option, Right, places " at the beginning of each entry and causes cell entries in the specified range to be right justified in the cells.

▶ /Range Name Create

Description: The /Range Name Create command allows you to assign names to cell ranges. Using names rather than cell addresses makes formulas easier to understand and helps you develop worksheet models that are self-documenting. Range names can be used anywhere cell addresses can be used.

Options: After entering /Range Name Create, you have two options: working with an existing range name or entering a new one. If you choose to work with an existing range name, you can select one of the names from the list of existing range names in the menu and have 1-2-3 highlight the cells that are currently assigned this name. At this point you can hit ESC to undo the existing range name assignment and specify a new range name.

To establish a new range name, after entering /Range Name Create, type a new range name of up to 15 characters and press ENTER. Next, respond to 1-2-3's prompt for the range by pointing to or entering a range and then pressing ENTER. The range name you choose should be as meaningful as possible.

1-2-3 does not restrict you to a single name for a given range of cells. If a range is used for more than one purpose, you can assign multiple names to it by using /Range Name Create a second time.

/Range Name Delete

Description: The /Range Name Delete command allows you to delete range names that you no longer need. Each execution of this command can remove a single range name. To delete a range name, enter /Range Name Delete, point to the appropriate name in the list 1-2-3 provides, and press ENTER. Or you can enter the command sequence, then type the name you wish to delete.

Options: None.

/Range Name Labels

Description: The /Range Name Labels command allows you to use label entries on the worksheet for range names in certain situations. With this command, each label can be assigned as a name only to a single cell. Furthermore, the name must be in a cell adjacent to the cell you wish to assign the name to. If you choose a label that exceeds the 15-character limit for range names, the label will be truncated. The /Range Name Labels command is most useful when you have a column or row of labels and wish to assign each one to the adjacent cell as a range name. A single execution of this command can assign all the range names.

Options: The /Range Name Labels command has four options — Right, Down, Up, and Left — which you select from a submenu. They tell 1-2-3 which direction to take in order to find the cell to apply the label to.

/Range Name Reset

Description: The /Range Name Reset command is equivalent to a "delete all" option. Rather than using /Range Name Delete to eliminate range names one by one, you can use this command to eliminate all range names with one command.

Options: None.

/Range Name Table

Description: The very useful /Range Name Table command is new under Release 2 of 1-2-3. With it you can obtain a list of all your range names and the range to which each name has been assigned. Before you execute this command, decide which area of your worksheet will be used to store the table of range names and assignments. After entering /Range Name Table, simply specify the table location. 1-2-3 will do the rest.

Options: The only options you have with this command are whether to specify the entire area for the table or to specify just the upper left cell in the table range. If you specify the entire range, 1-2-3 will not use additional space if the range is not large enough to contain all the entries. If you specify only the upper left corner, 1-2-3 will use as much space as required and will overwrite entries if the cells it uses contain other entries.

▶ /Range Protect

Description: The /Range Protect command is used for reprotecting cells that you have unprotected with the /Range Unprotect command. It allows you to change your mind and reestablish the protection features that are initially provided by 1-2-3 for every worksheet cell. Using the /Range Protect command has no apparent effect on a cell while the worksheet protection features are turned off. Once protection is turned 'on, however, cells that are protected will not accept entries of any type.

Since this command must be used in combination with /Worksheet Global Protection, read the entry for this command.

Options: The only options for this command are the variety of ways for entering the range once you have requested the command. You can type the range, use POINT mode to expand the cursor to include the entire range, or type the range name that you wish to use.

▶ /Range Transpose

Description: The /Range Transpose command is new in Release 2. It provides additional flexibility in restructuring a worksheet in that it will copy data from either a row or column orientation to the opposite orientation; that is, data stored in rows can be copied to columns, and vice versa. Note, however, that formulas in a transpose range may not be copied correctly, since 1-2-3 will not adjust relative cell references based on the new locations. You may want to consider freezing formulas to values with /Range Values before using this command or, alternatively, editing the formulas to change all the relative address references (such as T5 or A3) to absolute addresses (T5 or A3).

Options: The two options built into the command are selecting a From range with a row orientation, or selecting a From range with a column orientation. The choice is made not with a menu selection but rather with the entry of a cell range. 1-2-3 interprets this range as having either a row or a column orientation and produces a To range with the opposite orientation.

/Range Unprotect

Description: The /Range Unprotect command is used to change the cell-protection characteristics of a range of cells. Using this command will allow entries in the selected cells after worksheet-protection features are enabled.

Unless the /Range Unprotect option is used, all worksheet cells have a status of Protected. This means that entries cannot be made in the cells once the worksheet-protection features are enabled. To remove the protected status from a group of cells, simply enter /Range Unprotect and the range to unprotect.

Options: The only options for this command are the variety of ways for entering the range once you have requested the command. You can type the range, use POINT mode to expand the cursor to include the entire range, or type the range name that you wish to use.

/Range Value

Description: The /Range Value command is used to copy the values displayed by formula cells without copying the formulas. The cells containing the values can be copied to a different range on the worksheet or to the location containing the original formulas. In both cases, the cells copied to will not contain formulas, only the value result of the original formula.

Options: This command provides two options. When you enter /Range Value and specify the From range, you can specify a different To range to retain the original formulas and just make a copy of the values they contain, or you can specify the same range for To, thus eliminating the original formulas and retaining just the values.

▶ /System

Description: The /System command allows you to use the operating system commands without quitting 1-2-3. This means you can access some of the DOS commands while your 1-2-3 worksheet remains in memory. In order for you to use this command, Command.Com must be copied from your DOS disk to your 1-2-3 disk. The /System command is available only under release 2.

Options: Any DOS command that does not overlay memory can be used with /System. EXIT returns you to your worksheet.

▶ **/Worksheet Column**

Description: The /Worksheet Column command allows you to change the characteristics of the worksheet columns. You can use the command to change the column width and to hide and display columns.

Options: After entering /Worksheet Column, you will be presented with four options.

Set-Width: After choosing this option, you have two alternatives: Either use the RIGHT ARROW key and the LEFT ARROW key to change the column width of the current column, or type in the exact width desired for that column. With Release 1A, you can choose any width between 1 and 72. With Release 2, you can choose any width between 1 and 240. If you choose a column width narrower than the width of your data, numeric data will display as asterisks.

Reset-Width: This option returns the width setting for the current column to the default setting — that is, either the initial setting of nine characters or the setting established with /Worksheet Global Column-Width, if you used that command.

Hide: This option affects the display and printing of worksheet data. You can hide one or many columns, depending on the range you specify for this command. The hidden columns will not appear on your display. They also will not be printed, even if the print range spans cells on both sides of them.

This command will not affect the data in the cells. At any time you can bring the data back into view with the Display command.

Display: This command allows you to redisplay one or more hidden columns. Each hidden column will have an asterisk next to the column number. The columns can be redisplayed either by highlighting a cell within each column you wish to redisplay or by entering a range that includes the hidden columns you wish to redisplay.

▶ /Worksheet Delete

Description: The /Worksheet Delete command allows you to delete unneeded rows and columns. These rows or columns may be blank, or they may contain data. You can use this command to delete single or multiple rows and columns. Deletions from the middle of a range cause 1-2-3 to automatically adjust the range to compensate for the deletions.

Options: The /Range Delete command provides two options, Row and Column. You also have the option of deleting one or many rows or columns with a single execution of the command. The best approach is to place your cursor on the top row or left column to be deleted, enter /Worksheet Delete Row or /Worksheet Delete Column, and then expand your cursor to include all the rows or columns you wish to have deleted.

Note: A complete row or column must be deleted, since 1-2-3 does not provide an option for deleting part of a row or column.

▶ /Worksheet Erase

Description: The /Worksheet Erase command can be equivalent to a destroy instruction. It erases the working copy of your model from memory. Unless you have another copy of the worksheet stored on disk, you will not be able to retrieve the worksheet after using the /Worksheet Erase Yes option.

Options: The command presents a submenu with two options. One is Yes, which indicates that you want to proceed with the erasure of memory. The other, the default selection, is No, which abandons the erase operation.

▶ /Worksheet Global Column-Width

Description: The /Worksheet Global Column-

Width command allows you to change the default column width for every column on the worksheet.

Options: After entering /Worksheet Global Column-Width, either use the RIGHT ARROW key and the LEFT ARROW key to change the column width, or type in the exact width desired. With Release 1A, you can choose any width between 1 and 72. With Release 2, you can choose any width between 1 and 240.

▶ /Worksheet Global Default Directory

Description: This command permits you to specify the directory that 1-2-3 will automatically search for your files when it is loaded. Unless you change it, the default is drive A for Release 2 and drive B for Release 1A.

Options: Normally, when you enter /Worksheet Global Default Directory, you will enter a new default directory. A second option is to clear the existing entry without entering a new one. In this case, 1-2-3 will use the directory that was current when 1-2-3 was loaded as the default for file storage and retrieval.

Note: To make this directory change permanent, use /Worksheet Global Default Update to save the change to the file 123.CNF.

▷ /Worksheet Global Default Other Clock

Description: This command lets you display the format for the date and time in the left corner of your screen if you are using Release 2.

Options: This command provides three options.

Standard: This is the default setting. It displays the date in the format DD-MMM-YY and the time as HH:MM AM/PM.

International: This option displays the date in whichever long international format is in effect (month, day, and year will be shown) and the time in whichever short international format is in effect (hours and minutes, based on a 24-hour clock). The international format options are discussed in more detail under /Worksheet Global Default Other International.

None: This option suppresses the date and time display in the lower left corner of the screen.

▷ /Worksheet Global Default Other International

Description: The /Worksheet Global Default Other International command allows you to customize the display for numeric punctuation, currency, date, and time.

Options: The command has four options.

Punctuation: The numeric punctuation indicators you can control are the point separator (the decimal indicator in numbers such as 55.98), the thousands separator for numbers, and the argument separator used in functions. The initial point separator is a period (.), but you have the option of changing it to a comma (,). The initial thousands separator is a comma. It can be changed to a period (.) or a space. The argument separator is initially set as a comma. It can be changed to a period (.) or a semicolon (;). The options are not chosen individually but in a threesome, once you select Punctuation. The options available are shown in the following table:

Option	Point	Argument	Thousands
A	.	,	,
B	,	.	.
C	.	;	,
D	,	;	.
E	.	,	space
F	,	.	space
G	.	;	space
H	,	;	space

Currency: This option allows you to change the currency symbol from the standard $ to one of the international currency symbols found in the LICS codes. You can also use any of the other LICS codes if the currency symbol you want is not in the table. You have the further choice of placing the symbol at the end of your entry rather than at the beginning as in the initial setting.

To change the currency indicator, invoke /Worksheet Global Default International Currency and then use the Compose sequence to type the LICS code sequence, followed by ENTER. The Compose sequence allows you to enter more than one character in a single position. To access it, hold down the ALTERNATE key (ALT) while you press F1, then type the characters specified. For pounds, for example, you would type l followed by an equal sign.

Date: The international date formats (Date formats D4 and D5) can be altered with the Date option under the /Worksheet Global Default Other International command. The initial setting for the international date (option A) is MM/DD/YY. This can be changed to three other options, as follows:

B	DD/MM/YY
C	DD.MM.YY
D	YY-MM-DD

Time: You can change the appearance of the international time formats with this option. Format D8 shows hours, minutes, and seconds, while format D9 shows only hours and minutes. The initial international time setting (option A) is HH:MM:SS. The three options to which this setting can be changed are:

B	HH.MM.SS
C	HH,MM,SS
D	HHhMMmSSs

For example, using these settings to display the time for 12:30:25 PM. would cause the following results:

	D8	D9
A	12:30:25	12:30
B	12.30.25	12.30
C	12,30,25	12,30
D	12h30m25s	12h30m

▶ /Worksheet Global Default Printer

Description: This command allows you to change the default printer settings. These settings determine the way a document prints if you have not made particular specifications for it through the Print menu. They also determine the default interface between 1-2-3 and your printer. Changes made with this command are not permanent unless you save them with /Worksheet Global Default Update.

Options: The eleven options that follow are the ones presented with Release 2. The Interface options will be more limited if you are using an earlier release of 1-2-3. The last four Interface options, for local area network support, are available only in Release 2.

Interface: This option determines the type of connection between your printer and 1-2-3. There are three basic options with several choices: parallel connection, serial connection, or connection through a local area network. The available options are as follows:

(1)   Parallel (default setting)
(2)   Serial 1
(3)   Parallel 2
(4)   Serial 2
(5)   DOS device LPT1
(6)   DOS device LPT2
(7)   DOS device LPT3
(8)   DOS device LPT4

If you select one of the serial interface options, 1-2-3 will also ask you to specify a baud rate (the transmission speed it supports). For 110 baud you will have to set your printer at 2 stop bits, 8 bits, and no parity. For speeds other than 110, 1 stop bit will be sufficient.

Auto-LF: This option specifies whether your printer automatically issues line feeds after carriage returns. Installation sets this to correspond with your printer, although the initial setting is No, indicating that the printer does not automatically print line feeds. If you are getting double spacing on everything you print, set Auto-LF to Yes. If your paper is not advancing as it should, change this setting to No.

Left: This setting has a default value of 4, but you can change it to any number between 0 and 240.

Right: This setting has a default value of 76, but you can change it to any number between 0 and 240.

Top: This option has a default value of 2 but will accept values between 0 and 32.

Bottom: This option has a default setting of 2 but will accept values between 0 and 32.

Pg-Length: The default page length is 66, but in Release 2 it can be changed to any value between 10 and 100.

Wait: This option allows you to set the default for continuous or single-sheet-feed paper. The initial value is No, indicating continuous paper. If you change it to Yes for single sheets, it will cause 1-2-3 to wait after each page is printed.

Setup: This option specifies a string of control characters to be sent to your printer before every print request. The default is blank, indicating no print control codes. You may supply any valid control codes up to 39 characters in length. The control codes can be obtained from your printer manual. Precede each code with a backslash (\) and a zero.

Name: If you installed more than one text printer for 1-2-3, this option allows you to specify the printer to use. The initial value is the first printer selected during installation.

Quit: This option allows you to exit the Worksheet Global Default menu.

▶ /Worksheet Global Default Update

Description: The /Worksheet Global Default Update command allows you to save changes made to 1-2-3's default settings with the /Worksheet Global Default commands. This means that the new settings will be available the next time you work with 1-2-3. The settings will be saved in the 123.CNF file on your 1-2-3 disk.

Options: None.

▶ /Worksheet Global Format

Description: The /Worksheet Global Format command allows you to change the default display format for the entire worksheet. All numeric entries on the worksheet will use the format chosen with this command unless they have been formatted with the /Range Format command, which has priority over /Worksheet Global Format.

Options: To define your format selection, you have ten menu options.

Fixed: Fixed format allows you to display all entries with a specific number of decimal places. Two places are the default, but you may select any number between 0 and 15. Examples with three decimal places are .007, 9.000, and 4.156.

Scientific: Scientific format displays numbers in exponential form, showing the power of 10 that the number must be multiplied by. This format allows you to concisely represent very large or very small numbers. From 0 to 15 places can be specified for the multiplier. Some examples with two decimal places are 6.78E–20, 4.11E+5, and 0.78E+8.

Currency: Currency format will cause your entries to be preceded by a dollar sign ($). It will also insert a separator such as a comma between the thousands and hundreds positions. You may specify from 0 to 15 decimal places for the Currency format; 2 is the default. Negative amounts will appear in parentheses. Examples with two decimal places are $3.40, $1,400.98, and ($89.95).

, (Comma): Comma format is identical to the Currency format, except that Comma lacks the dollar sign ($). Comma format uses the thousands separator and allows you to specify the number of decimal places you want between 0 and 15. Two decimal places are the default. Negative numbers are displayed in parentheses. Examples with two decimal places are 1,200.00, (5,678.00), and 45.00.

General: General is the default format for 1-2-3. With it the leading zero integer will always appear, as in 0.78, but trailing zeros will be suppressed. If the number is very large or very small, it will appear in scientific notation. Examples of numeric displays with the General format are 15.674, 2.7E+12, and 0.67543.

+/‑ format: This format produces a horizontal bar graph showing the relative size of numbers. Each integer is represented by a symbol. For example –3 would be –––, and 5 would be +++++. A . is used to represent 0.

Percent: Percent format displays your entries as percentages. Each entry will be multiplied by 100, and a % symbol will be added to the end. Because of this multiplication, you must enter percents as their decimal equivalent. For example, you must enter .05 for 5%. If you enter 5 and format the cell as Percent, it will display as 500%. You may specify from 0 to 15 decimal places; 2 is the default. Examples with two decimal places are 4.00%, 3.15%, and 1200.00%.

Date: The Date option is the only format choice that provides a second menu of possibilities. From this second menu you can select specific formats for the date. The formats accessible through the date option are as follows:

D1	(DD-MMM-YY)	08-Sep-86
D2	(DD-MMM)	08-Sep
D3	(MMM-YY)	Sep-86
D4	(MM/DD/YY)	09/08/86
D5	(MM/DD)	09/08

In Release 2, Time formats are accessed through the Date format. When you select Time from the Date format options, a menu of four time formats will be presented. Two of the formats use the AM and PM designation, and the other two are international formats that use a 24-hour day, like military time. The formats available for the display of time in your worksheet cells are:

(D6) T1	HH:MM:SS AM/PM	06:00:00 AM
(D7) T2	HH:MM AM/PM	06:00 AM
(D8) T3	Long International	06:00:00 *
(D9) T4	Short International	06:00 *

* This format can be changed to a number of options with the /Worksheet Global Default Other International command.

Text: Text format displays the cells selected exactly as you have entered them. In the case of formulas, the formula rather than the result will be displayed.

Hidden: Hidden format causes the selected cells to appear blank on the screen. If you move your cursor to one of these cells, the control panel will display the entry you made in the cell.

▶ /Worksheet Global Label-Prefix

Description: The /Worksheet Global Label-Prefix command allows you to change the default prefix, and therefore the justification (placement in the cell), for all label entries on the worksheet. Entries made prior to the use of this command will retain their original label indicators and their existing justification. Entries made in any cell after the command is used will have the new label indicator at the front of the entry.

Options: This command has three options: Left, Right, and Center. Left generates a ' as the label prefix; Right generates a " and Center generates a ^ at the beginning of each label entry.

Note: This command takes a different approach from that of the /Range Label command, which changes the label indicator and justification for existing entries but does not affect entries into cells within the range that have not yet been made. Entries made after you have used /Range Label will use the default label prefix.

/Worksheet Global Protection

Description: The /Worksheet Global Protection command allows you to turn the protection features on for all worksheet cells that are protected. This command is also used to disable protection for the entire worksheet. The command works with the /Range Protect feature to determine which worksheet cells are protected and which are unprotected. If this command is used to enable protection for a new worksheet, you will not be able to make entries in any worksheet cells, since all the cells have a default status of Protected.

Once protection has been enabled, you will see a PR in the control panel when your cursor is in cells that are protected. The color and highlighting created with the / Range Unprotect command is maintained. With a color monitor, unprotected cells are highlighted in green, providing a "green light" signal that you can proceed with entries for that cell. Other cells remain their normal color. With a monochrome display, the unprotected cells are highlighted to indicate that you can make entries in these cells.

Options: This command has two options. The first is Enable, which turns on protection for the entire worksheet. Entering /Worksheet Global Protection Enable will prevent entries to cells that have a Protected status and allow entries only to those cells that have a status of Unprotected.

The second option is Disable. This option turns off protection for the entire worksheet and permits entries to all cells. You can use this command to temporarily turn off protection so that you can modify a formula, erase or delete worksheet entries, or unprotect some of the worksheet cells.

Note: You must use the / Range Unprotect command before you enable protection. Otherwise, you will be locked out of all worksheet cells.

▶ /Worksheet Global Recalculation

Description: This command provides access to all the recalculation options. With the use of / Worksheet Global Recalculation you can affect the number of recalculations for a worksheet, determine whether the recalculation is automatic, and specify the order in which formulas are recalculated.

Options: The six options for this command affect three different features of recalculation.

Automatic: This option causes the worksheet to recalculate automatically after every worksheet entry.

Manual: This option turns off the automatic recalculation feature.

Natural: This option places the responsibility for determining which formula to evaluate first with 1-2-3.

Rowwise: This option disables the natural recalculation sequence and switches to recalculation by rows.

Columnwise: This option disables the natural recalculation sequence and switches to recalculation by columns.

Iterations: The normal setting for this option is 1, meaning that every formula is recalculated once during every recalculation. You can reset it by typing in the number of iterations you want.

/Worksheet Insert

Description: You can use the /Worksheet Insert command to add blank rows and columns to your worksheet. These blank areas can be used to improve readability or to allow for the addition of new information to your worksheet.

Inserts made to the middle of a range of cells will automatically expand the reference for a range name applied to those cells. The same is true for formulas that reference this range; they will automatically be expanded to allow for the additional rows or columns.

Options: This command provides two options, Rows and Columns, which you can select from a menu. Columns are always added to the left of the cursor location or the range you specify. Rows are always added above the cursor or the range you specify.

/Worksheet Global Zero

Description: This command allows you to suppress

the display of cells that have a value equal to zero. It is available only under Release 2.

Options: The /Worksheet Global Zero Command presents only two options: Yes and No. The default is No, which allows zero values to display. Choosing the Yes option will suppress the display of zero values.

▶ /Worksheet Status

Description: This command provides a screen snapshot of your current worksheet environment. It allows you to monitor available memory as well as many of the default worksheet settings. You cannot make changes to any of the settings from this screen.

Options: In one sense there are no options for this command, since /Worksheet Status has no submenu. However, a variety of information is presented on the status screen. Even though the different items cannot be selected individually, they can be regarded as options.

Available Memory: This portion of the display reports on the amount of available memory that you have used. Conventional and expanded memory are shown separately. This information helps you plan the remainder of your worksheet entries. If memory is almost fully used, you may have to split your worksheet in two.

Math Coprocessor: Release 2 supports the use of a math coprocessor chip. This item on the status screen reports whether one of the supported chips is installed in your system.

Recalculation: This section reports all the recalculation options. You can tell whether recalculation is set at Automatic or Manual. You can also see whether the current recalculation order is set at Natural, Rowwise, or Columnwise. The current number of iterations of recalculation is also displayed. To make changes to any of the recalculation options, you must use / Worksheet Global Recalculation.

Circular Reference: Anyone who has struggled to find a circular reference in earlier releases of 1-2-3 will appreciate this display. It shows you the address of the cell causing the CIRC indicator to appear at the bottom of your screen.

Cell Display: This section of the status screen provides four different pieces of information: the global format settings, the current default label prefix, the current default column width, and whether zero suppression is turned on or off. You can make changes to format with / Worksheet

Global Format. The label prefix is changed with /Worksheet Global Label-Prefix. Changes to column width are made with /Worksheet Global Column-Width. Changes to zero suppression are made with /Worksheet Global Zero.

Global Protection: The last area of the status screen shows whether global protection is enabled or disabled. Changes to the protection status can be made with /Worksheet Global Protection.

▶ /Worksheet Titles

Description: The /Worksheet Titles command allows you to freeze label information at the top or left side of the screen. This is useful when you have a worksheet that is either wider or longer than the screen. Without the titles frozen on the screen, you would not have any descriptive information. The cursor-movement keys will not move your cursor to the titles area once it is frozen on the screen. If you want to move there, you will have to use the F5 (GOTO) key, which will cause the title area to be shown on the screen twice. When you scroll away from this area, the double view of the titles will disappear from the screen.

Options: There are four options for this command.

Both: This command freezes information above and to the left of the cursor on your screen.

Horizontal: This command freezes information above the cursor on your screen.

Vertical: This option freezes information to the left of the cursor on your screen.

Clear: This option eliminates freezing of titles.

▶ /Worksheet Window

Description: The /Worksheet Window command allows you to create two separate windows on your screen. This has advantages for large worksheets where you cannot view the entire worksheet on one screen. You can view two different sections of the worksheet through the two windows created by this command. The windows' size is controlled by the location of your cursor at the time you request the screen split. When the screen is split vertically, a dividing line will replace one of the worksheet columns; when it is split horizontally, the dividing line will replace one of the rows. You can move easily between windows with the F6 (WINDOW) key. The F6 key always moves you to the window opposite the one you are in.

Options: There are five options for the Window command. One clears (removes) the extra window, two control the type of window, and two control data movement within the windows.

Horizontal: This option splits the screen into two horizontal windows. The dividing line is inserted immediately above the cursor.

Vertical: This option splits the screen into two vertical windows. The dividing line is inserted immediately to the left of the cursor.

Sync: This option causes scrolling in the two windows to be synchronized. That is, when you scroll in one window, the other window will automatically scroll along with it. This is the default setting when you create a second window.

Unsync: This option allows you to scroll in one window while the other window remains stationary.

Clear: This option removes the second window from the screen. The window that remains will be the top window if the split was horizontal and the left window if the split was vertical.

PRINTGRAPH COMMANDS

▶ PrintGraph Align

Description: The PrintGraph Align command tells 1-2-3 that you have your printer paper at the top of a form.

Options: None.

▶ PrintGraph Exit

Description: A selection of Exit from the Print-Graph menu exits the PrintGraph program.

Options: None.

▶ PrintGraph Go

Description: Selecting PrintGraph Go will cause 1-2-3 to print the graphs chosen with Image-Select. The settings selected on the PrintGraph menu will be used when printing the selected graphs. Pressing CTRL-BREAK will stop the printing of a graph as soon as the printer buffer is empty. When a plotter is specified as the device, you will receive a message prompting you to change plotter pens.

Options: None.

▶ PrintGraph Image-Select

Description: Image-Select will present a list of all the .PIC files in the directory established as the graphs directory. The default setting for this directory is A:\. You can select files by pointing to them and pressing the space bar to mark the file names with a #. You can choose as many files as you wish. Your selection order will control the print order when Go is selected.

Options: If you press F10 while pointing to a file name, 1-2-3 will display the graph on your screen.

▶ PrintGraph Page

Description: This command advances the paper in your printer by the number of lines in one page.

Options: None.

▶ PrintGraph Settings Action

Description: This command allows you to determine the actions that PrintGraph will take after each graph is printed.

Options: This command has three options.

Pause: When this option is set to Yes, Print-Graph will pause for a paper change between graphs. When it is set to No, PrintGraph expects continuous forms and will continue printing graphs without pause.

Eject: When set to Yes, this option ejects the page after each graph is printed. When this option is set to No, PrintGraph will print two half-page graphs on one page.

Quit: The Quit option returns you to the Settings menu.

▶ PrintGraph Settings Hardware

Description: The Settings Hardware option provides access to the commands that change graph and font directories, the interface with the printer or plotter, the print device, and the paper size.

Options: There are six options for this command.

Graphs-Directory: This option allows you to specify the pathname for the .PIC files that you plan to print.

Fonts-Directory: This option allows you to specify the pathname for the .FNT files that contain the fonts PrintGraph will need to produce your graphs.

Interface: This option defines the type of connection between your system and your printer or plotter (serial, parallel, or local area network device).

Printer: This option permits you to select one of the graphics printers defined during installation.

Page-Size: This option permits you to define the length and width of the paper you are using.

Quit: This option returns you to the Settings menu.

▶ PrintGraph Settings Image

Description: The Settings Image command permits you to determine the appearance of the graphics image. You can choose fonts, size, and range colors with this command.

Options: PrintGraph Settings Image has four options.

Size: This option lets you choose a full-page graph, a half-page graph, and manual page-size definition. It also lets you rotate the graph from 0 to 90 degrees before printing. The Manual option has a separate submenu.

Font: This option permits you to select either one or two fonts from a list of fonts displayed by PrintGraph. Fonts with a 2 after the font name will be darker than fonts with a 1. The first font you specify will be used for the first title of the graph, and the second font will be used for the remainder of the text.

Range-Colors: With this option you can choose ranges from A through F or X and select a color for each range by either highlighting the color name or typing the first character of the name. Naturally, this command will be effective only if you have a color printer or a plotter.

Quit: This option returns you to the settings menu.

▶ PrintGraph Settings Quit

Description: Selecting the Quit option from the Settings menu returns you to the main Print-Graph menu.

Options: None.

▶ PrintGraph Settings Reset

Description: The Settings Reset command returns your settings to the ones in the PGRAPH.CNF file (the default settings).

Options: None.

▶ PrintGraph Settings Save

Description: This command saves the current settings in the PGRAPH.CNF file, making them the default settings for all subsequent sessions.

Options: None.

BUILT-IN FUNCTIONS

This is a comprehensive list of all the 1-2-3 functions. Functions which are only available in Release 2 and 2.01 are marked with a bullet (•).

@@(cell) •
@ABS(number)
@ACOS(number)
@ASIN(number)
@ATAN(number)
@ATAN2(number)
@AVG(list)
@CELL(attribute string,range) •
@CELLPOINTER(attribute string) •
@CHAR(code) •
@CHOOSE(number,list)
@CLEAN(string) •
@CODE(string) •
@COLS(range) •
@COS(number)
@COUNT(list)
@CTERM(interest,future value,present value) •
@DATE(year,month,day)
@DATEVALUE(date string) •
@DAVG(input range,offset column,criteria range)
@DAY(serial date number)
@DCOUNT(input range,offset column,criteria range)
@DDB(cost,salvage,life,period) •
@DMAX(input range,offset column,criteria range)

@DMIN(input range,offset column,criteria range)
@DSTD(input range,offset column,criteria range)
@DSUM(input range,offset column,criteria range)
@DVAR(input range,offset column,criteria range)
@ERR
@EXACT(string1,string2) •
@EXP(number)
@FALSE
@FIND(search string,entire string,starting
   location) •
@FV(payment,interest,term)
@HLOOKUP(code to be looked up,table location,
   offset)
@HOUR(serial time number)
@IF(condition to be tested,value if true,value if
   false)
@INDEX(table location,column number,row
   number)
@INT(number)
@IRR(guess,range)
@ISERR(value)
@ISNA(value)
@ISNUMBER(value)
@ISSTRING(number) •
@LEFT(string,number of characters to be ex-
   tracted) •
@LENGTH(string) •
@LN(number)
@LOG(number)
@LOWER(string) •
@MAX(list)

@MID(string,start number,number of characters) •
@MIN(list)
@MINUTE(serial time number) •
@MOD(number,divisor)
@MONTH(serial date number)
@N(range) •
@NA
@NOW •
@NPV(discount rate,range)
@PI
@PMT(principal,interest,term of loan)
@PROPER(string) •
@PV(payment,periodic interest rate,number of periods)
@RAND
@RATE(future value,present value,number of periods) •
@REPEAT(string,number of times) •
@REPLACE(original string,start location,# characters, new string) •
@RIGHT(string,number of characters to be extracted) •
@ROUND(number to be rounded,place of rounding)
@ROWS(range) •
@S(range) •
@SECOND(serial time number) •
@SIN(number)
@SLN(cost,salvage value,life of the asset) •
@SQRT(number)
@STD(list)

@STRING(number,number of decimal places) •
@SUM(list)
@SYD(cost,salvage value,life,period) •
@TAN(number)
@TERM(payment,interest,future value) •
@TIME(hour,minute,second) •
@TIMEVALUE(time string) •
@TODAY
@TRIM(string) •
@TRUE
@UPPER(string) •
@VALUE(string) •
@VAR(list)
@VLOOKUP(code to be looked up,table location,
   offset)
@YEAR(serial date number)

MACRO LANGUAGE COMMANDS

{?}: accepts keyboard input

{**BEEP pitch level**}: sounds bell

{**BLANK location**}: erases cell or range

{**BRANCH location**}: changes execution flow to a new macro instruction

{**BREAKOFF**}: disables BREAK key

{**BREAKON**}: restores BREAK key function

{**CLOSE**}: closes an open file

{**CONTENTS destination,source,width,format**}: stores the numeric contents of a cell as a label in another cell

{**DEFINE location1:type1..locationn,typen**}: specifies location and type of arguments for a subroutine call

{**DISPATCH location**}: branches to a new location indirectly

{**FILESIZE location**}: determines number of bytes in a file

{**FOR ctr,start,stop,increment,startloc**}: loops through a macro subroutine multiple times

{**FORBREAK**}: cancels current {FOR} instruction

{**GET location**}: halts macro to allow single-keystroke entry

{**GETLABEL prompt message, location**}: halts macro to allow label entry

{**GETNUMBER prompt message, location**}: halts macro to allow number entry

{GETPOS location}: returns pointer position in a file

{IF condition}: causes conditional execution of command that follows

{INDICATE mode indicator}: changes mode indicator

{LET location, string}: stores a number or label in a cell

{LOOK location}: checks to see if entry has been made

{MENUBRANCH location}: branches to a customized menu

{MENUCALL location}: executes a customized menu as a subroutine

{ONERROR location}: branches to an error-processing routine

{OPEN file,access}: opens a file for read or write access

{PANELOFF}: eliminates control panel updating

{PANELON}: restores control panel updating

{PUT location,column,row,number}: stores a number or label in one cell of a range

{QUIT}: ends the macro and returns to READY mode

{READ bytes,location}: reads characters from file into cell

{READLN location}: reads a line of characters from a file

{RECALC location,condition,iteration}: recalculates formulas in a range row by row

{RECALCCOL location,condition,iteration}: re calculates formulas in a range column by column

{RESTART}: clears subroutine pointers

{RETURN}: routines to the instruction after the last subroutine call or {MENUCALL}

{routine}: calls the subroutine specified by routine

{SETPOS number}: moves file pointer to a new location in the file

{WAIT time_serial_number}: waits until a specified time

{WINDOWSOFF}: suppresses window updating

{WINDOWSON}: restores window updating

{WRITE string}: places data in a file

{WRITELN string}: places data in file and adds a carriage return/line feed at the end

/XC: calls a subroutine

/XG: branches to a new location

/XI: tests a logical condition

/XL: gets a label entry from the keyboard

/XM: creates a user-defined menu

/XN: gets a number from the keyboard

/XQ: quits the macro

/XR: returns control to the main macro code from a subroutine

SPECIAL KEYS IN MACRO COMMANDS

1-2-3 has a keyword to represent each of the special keyboard keys, except for the NUM LOCK key and the SCROLL LOCK key. The keyword symbol for each of the keys is shown in the following table.

Cursor Movement Keys	Keywords
Up arrow	{UP}
Down arrow	{DOWN}
Right arrow	{RIGHT}
Left arrow	{LEFT}
HOME	{HOME}
END	{END}
PGUP	{PGUP}
PGDN	{PGDN}
CTRL-RIGHT	{BIGRIGHT}
CTRL-LEFT	{BIGLEFT}

Editing Keys	
DEL	{DEL} or {DELETE}
INS	{INSERT}
ESC	{ESC} or {ESCAPE}
BACKSPACE	{BACKSPACE} or {BS}

Function Keys

F2 (EDIT)	{EDIT}
F3 (NAME)	{NAME}
F4 (ABS)	{ABS}
F5 (GOTO)	{GOTO}
F6 (WINDOW)	{WINDOW}
F7 (QUERY)	{QUERY}
F8 (TABLE)	{TABLE}
F9 (CALC)	{CALC}
F10 (GRAPH)	{GRAPH}

Special Keys

Input from keyboard during macro	{?}
ENTER key	~
Tilde	{~}
{	{{}
}	{}}

FUNCTION KEYS

F1	Help
Alt F1	Compose
F2	Edit
Alt	F2 Step mode
F3	Name
F4	Absolute value
F5	Go to
F6	Window
F7	Query
F8	Table
F9	Calc
F10	Graph

MOVING AROUND
ON THE WORKSHEET

In READY mode

→	Moves one character to the right
←	Moves one character to the left
↑	Moves up one row
↓	Moves down one row
Ctrl + →	Scrolls a screen to the right
Ctrl + ←	Scrolls a screen to the left
Home	Moves the cell pointer to A1
End	Moves to the last entry in the direction specified by the arrow key which follows it.

In EDIT mode

→	Moves one character to the right
←	Moves one character to the left
Home	Moves to the beginning of the entry on the edit line
End	Moves to the end of the entry on the edit line
Tab	Moves five characters to the right on the edit line
Shift Tab	Moves five characters to the left on the edit line

In MENU mode

→	Moves to the next menu selection
←	Moves to the previous menu selection
Home	Moves to the first menu selection
End	Moves to the last menu selection